100
YEARS

NATHAN
BROWN

MEZCALITA
PRESS

MEZCALITA PRESS, LLC
Norman, Oklahoma

MEZCALITA PRESS, LLC
Norman, Oklahoma

100
YEARS

NATHAN BROWN

TABLE OF CONTENTS

ACKNOWLEDGEMENTS

Thanks to Sandi Horton and the *WordFest Anthology 2018* of the Waco Cultural Arts Fest for first publishing the poem "83 – The Baker."

Thanks to Dorothy Alexander for publishing the poem "84 – Who's to Judge" in *Speak Your Mind: Poems in Defense of Freedom*, the 2019 anthology for the Woody Guthrie Festival. (Village Books Press.)

And thanks to George Bilgere, Ben Myers, and Milton Brasher-Cunningham for reading through these and making me feel like they liked them.

Also, I want to send a thank you to the community of authors here at Mezcalita Press who are building a team dedicated to bringing the good stuff.

Many thanks to my parents, Lavonn and Norma Brown, for being the great supporters of the arts they are… as well as the inspiration for key poems in this book. You are why I've been able to do this.

Sierra… my daughter… my moon child… you are in here as well… as well as always in my heart.

Ashley… my wife… you are in all my poems. Thank you, Babe, for hanging in there with me.

100

YEARS

0 – Chubby Butts and Pink Hands

Toward the end
of that first year,
something tells us
our better days are
likely behind us now.

We've had a good run,
but it feels like it is time
to learn to lift our chubby
little butts off the floor…
since no one pinches 'em
while cooing anymore…

then raise our pink hands
in the air around our heads,
in rehearsal for that first arrest…
a minor offense, or misdemeanor…

and finally take those initial hard steps,
the beginning of our walking away
from everything that is safe…

the great migration to all
that is foreign.

1 – TURNING THE PAGE

Her world is the twirl
and swirl of butterflies,
and all the fluttery things
that look so much like them.

It's a floor full of bright toys,
a blossoming of imagination
in an absence of little boys.

It means to triple in size,
to stand on her own feet.

It is that first taste of honey,
to turn the book's page herself.

It is to get the food in the spoon,
then learn how to aim that thing.

And to say "No" to cauliflower,
as well as the outstretched arms
of strangers, one of those *others*
she's never really cared for,
now that she has a say
in the matter.

2 – IT FALLS APART

It shocked the system
when he first began to realize
that not every little noise he made,

not all of the pees he peed…
or poops he pooped…
were cute, or funny,

to those who followed
around behind him all day
with Lysol and Handi Wipes.

Till now, his narcissism had
worked like the well-oiled
machine nature intended.

But, the maintenance crew
hasn't had a wink of sleep
in a couple of years now.

Their eyes have changed.
And they don't chuckle
as much as they used to.

And so the whole scene
just makes him want
to cry and scream.

3 – PRACTICE, PRACTICE

Why is the sky blue,
   except when it's not?
Why does the cat
   have feathers in its mouth?
Why do some eggs
   not become chickens?
Why is dad gone so much?
Why can't we eat cookies
   for breakfast every morning?
Why does that man
   sleep on the sidewalk?
Why does broccoli taste
   and feel like eating a tree?
Why does God never ever laugh?
Why do cookies taste
   so much better than broccoli?
Why did God create
   broccoli to begin with?
Why were your eyes so red
   when you came out of the bathroom?
Why does the dog
   get to poop in the yard?
Why does dad yell at the TV
   when he comes home at night?
Why do boys look like that down there?
Why doesn't Lucy let Charlie Brown
   kick that silly football?

4 – THE SHAPE OF THINGS

He's looking
for the shape
of something
in the Play-Doh...

pinching bits of it
off of one side,
sticking them
to the other...

a bubble here,
thumb-dent there,
he is never quite
satisfied, and...

he'll be looking
for the shape
of something
the rest of his life.

But we don't need
to tell him now.

5 – NOT THIS

She sits, with a plastic cup of water,
arms folded, at a table by herself…

in Starbucks, staring out and way off
into the polluted light of the suburbs.

Grandmother sips a caramel mocha
at a table nearby, wearing a pair of
Jackie O sunglasses while tapping
the screen of a leopard-print phone
with a single and very long fingernail,

apparently oblivious to the last thing
a five-year-old girl would want to do.

And that little thousand-year stare
proves she is much closer to six
than she is four, and that she's
already developing a stance
on what she does not
want in life.

6 – MAKING HONEY

~ in honor of Dr. Seuss

He's only six years old.
So why on earth would it be
they feel the need to speak of
this bird and some stupid bee?

If actually they want to tell him
of men and women, and babies,
then please don't tell by way of
these birds and some stupid bees.

If sex is on their grown-up minds,
then they must find better words
than these ridiculous musings
on sex and bees and birds.

So yes, if honey comes from
this act among buzzing insects,
then please just let them be. Yes,
let them bees have plenty of sex.

7 – POWER SHIFT

Jenny's new to the scene,
but she soon figured out
that Ben was the cool one.
Not mean. It's just that he
sort of runs the show here.

But, it's not her fault that—
when it comes to armpit farts—
hers are a lot longer and louder.

So things got a little too quiet
when she let that first one rip.
Yet two of the boys in the clan
couldn't keep from laughing,
because it was so awesome.
But Ben seemed unnerved
by the competition—kids
looked around at each other
or pretended to clean a shoe
on one of the swing-set poles.

She had never stopped to think
that a simple skill could screw with
the social structure of the playground.
But later, in the lunchroom, when
she let loose a burp as big
as a drunken sailor…
even Ben laughed.

8 - MARIA

She never felt fear
before their mama died.
Only after her older brother
began to talk about the "trip"
they'd soon have to make.

She heard whispers late
into the night between
her aunt and uncle…

so many *yeses* and *noes*,
she couldn't tell which
was going to be the one.

But her brother assured her
they had friends on the other
side of some river nearby.
All they have to do is
get to the far shore.

There is a fence.
But he has a plan.

* ~ *

The water was frigid.
Her clothes grew hard,

and caught on the razor wire.
It sliced her thigh just below
her right hip, and she began
to cry, silently, in the long
hours of their walking.

*   ~   *

The darkness was so dark,
the blast of headlight beams
first felt something like hope,
an almost warmth to the glow.

And the uniforms crisscrossing
the bright rays in a cloud of dust
had an air of rescue about them.

But the voices... voices dark
as the night around them...
brought back the fear.

9 – ALL SO NEW

He likes his new friend, Zak,
who has a strange, easy-going
confidence in the way he walks
—and the way that he talks about
the mysteries of a world out there
—as if other places might exist.

They met in the new halls of their
new school because their old town
tore down the one covered in mold
and lead-based paint, and because
he was lost and Zak... somehow...
seemed to know where he was going.

And he didn't know why he'd never
seen Zak before. Nothing and no one
new ever happened or came to this town.
And he didn't know why someone like Zak
would invite someone like him over to play
at his family's big and very-new house.

And he couldn't figure out how
Zak's parents could be so cool
and funny, or how his big sister
could be so cool and pretty both.
It was all just... so... new to a kid
who lived in such an old, old town.

And when they sat down to dinner,
both of Zak's parents served real food
that both of Zak's parents had cooked.
And Zak and his sister sat right next
to each other and didn't even fight.
More newness than he could take.

But still he sat next to his new friend
in his new friend's new home, feeling
something new and strange for his new
friend's big sister… while eating all these
new kinds of food and began to wonder
how he might make this his new family.

10 – THE FLIP OF A SWITCH

Within days of turning ten,
her right fist shot up
to her right hip…

with the right elbow
pulled notably forward.

And, it has not been seen
to relax for one minute since.

To go along with that,
her eyes have taken
to rolling upwards…

with the drama and force
of a titan's blazing chariot
dragging the sun behind it.

And since her voice is steadily
rising in pitch and volume,
everyone else in the house
feels like a hostage now.

All waiting, nervously…
to see how this pans out.

11 – THE ANSWER TO THE PROBLEM

They learned addition
years ago. And since
she now knows that
anything times zero
always equals zero,

it's not all that hard
to figure out where
this whole school
thing is headed.

She'll be filling in
circles with a No. 2
lead pencil for about
seven or more years.

And so, since Carson
has been making eyes
at her all first period,
she's decided maybe
the next little circle
she'll shade in…

is going to be ©

12 – LITTLE MURDERS

There are a thousand ways
a seventh-grade girl gets lost.

Sometimes at the stinger-end
of a single comment, a vicious

stare. Are we somehow taught
to perform these early cruelties?

Or, is it some nasty chromosome
we need to find and try to defuse?

Either way… adults need to listen
hard and close to all of the things

she will not say. For there are little
murders she's leaving uncommitted

every other day, little half-thought
thoughts that are as treacherous

as any knife, or small handgun,
snuck into school in a backpack.

She needs bigger people to hear
the screams inside her silences.

13 – Required Silence

A 13-year-old boy learns to contain
any excitement he may feel toward
his card collection, Christmas gifts,
or especially Spiderman—the death

that occurs between 7th and 8th grade.
A death that breaks any parent's heart.
Any parent who pays attention and sees
the moment the light passes from his eyes,

leaving us all missing now our sweet little
pain in the ass who whined in the aisles
of Target because he was going to Die!
without the newer Batman action figure.

He'll dive, and run silent, for the required
amount of time, till some sort of graduation.
Then, if he's lucky, his passions will return.
If not... he will become a tax accountant.

14 – OUR KEEPERS

At 14, the ol' girl's old enough
to know that she is supposed
to die before the human does.

Every breed understands this…
though, she wonders sometimes
about those Beagles and Bulldogs.

That's why the absence of kibble
and her leash this morning
caught her off guard.

And so, when she went back
to the master bedroom, sniffed…
then licked the cold hand, she began

the nervous circle-dance of, "This
is *not* how it works. No. This is
not the order of things…"

15 – IGNITION

Is there anyone as wonderfully lonely
as a 15-year-old boy who loves books
and baking—and happens also to be
deeply, if not frighteningly, self-aware?

No one understands what he isn't saying
in the halls of his school where his parents
—hell... even the principal—are wishing
he'd get into more trouble than he does.

But why should he be blamed for refusing
to remain stupid for the rest of his life—
like most other students... and teachers,
for that matter, except maybe Ms. St. John.

She sees it... and has all along... that he
could, would, and should never be, like
the others. So... she runs interference
for him, silently, and behind the scenes.

She knows from experience what happens
when all those sparks collide into flames.

16 – SO…

What is SO wonderful
about the great big world
out there waiting for her?

She likes her bedroom. So…
so what if she wants to stay
holed up in it all the time?

Being thoroughly left alone
requires just as much skill as, say,
turning back flips on a football field.

Besides, she's old enough to know,
at this point in the stupid game,
what she's not cut out for. So…

so she wants to be in this house.
She wants this bed, by that chair,
and the tiny desk that goes with it.

And while she's at it, by the way,
she's hoping to raise her future
kids right here in it too. So…

so as far as she is concerned,
her parents can just go ahead
and sign the deed over now.

17 – He Knows

Graduating won't solve
an East Los Angeles
kind of problem.

Leaving's what he needs.
And… he knows it…
and so does mom.

But leaving requires
a set of wheels…
or a bus ticket.

And he knows a ticket
costs a lot less…
that is, until

you get where you're going
and then have no way
to get around.

And mom thinks graduating
will help him. Though,
she understands

that leaving might actually
be more important
at this point,

at least with the latest round
of deadly drive-bys
in the hood.

And he knows that buying
a set of wheels is not
an option for him,

or her, for that matter. So,
the only other way
to get one…

is something else
he knows.

18 – Not Getting It

At 18, six eggs every morning
and a steady course of steroids
got him all the way to Captain of
a Triple A high school football team.

Biceps that look like grapefruit implants.
His thighs the size of telephone poles.

Muscles that do most of his mind's
heavy lifting, so that all that gray
matter in there can stay off on
an extended spring vacation.

He smiles beneath creased hair
behind the counter of the town's
only coffee shop where a notable
number of high school girls enjoy
looking over the tops of iced mocha
lattes, minus the whip, which would be
over the top on sexual connotation.

Which they just do not get
that he wouldn't get.

19 – THE WRONG THING

At 19, she's confused… a bit
disappointed in herself, really.

She had done all of the things
she's supposed to do to baffle
and terrorize the sad parents—
the green and the purple streaks
in her once beautiful black hair…
the nose ring, an ugly ankle tattoo.

Even all the yelling and screaming
between bouts of totally not caring.
Hours upon hours of dark brooding,
day after day of hard nonstop blasting
of her favorites, Avenged Sevenfold.

But still… there he stands… almost
every afternoon… right next to, and
all around her at the stained counter
in the coffee shop where they work
together… the oh so awfully, and
absolutely, Wrong Thing for her:
the captain of the football team.

And she is, sadly…
yet madly…
in love.

20 – MOON CHILD

She fled the suburbs,
that hostessing job, and
the money that went with it,
in a red broken-down Subaru
driven by a set of dreadlocks.

Her own dreads had already
sprung up all over her head,
and she's eight months now
into the cañons and arroyos
of Northern New Mexico,

    a Mountain Princess…
        an Earth Warrior…
            a Moon Child…

Star Seed, learning to grow
tomatoes and squash while
picking wild blackberries…
and trimming pot of course.

The gemstones sing to her…
    the Tarot deck guides her…
        and the Ayahuasca has
        permanently altered her
        perception of the universe.

And she may not save the world,

but she'll do a helluva better job
trying than Republicans ever will.

And she'll stop shoving plastic shit
down the throat of Mother Earth.

And she will kneel to drink from
the underground springs that
haven't yet been tainted.

And… she will not
be coming home
any time soon.

21 – Taking Steps

It started with only a couple of snips
along the outer edge of each nostril,
a gift she gave herself for turning 21.

But, she did not bother with reasons
when she went back to the same clinic
to get her trans-umbilical breast implants.

From there she took things into her own
hands… and… much more than words
came out of her mouth after any meal.

Some days she nets a mere 100 calories,
working like a terrorist alone in a basement
to decrease herself in the eyes of the world.

And there are levels of sadness that do not
register on any scale known to the DSM-5
Diagnostic and Statistical Manual's 992

pages. Any psychiatrist can tell you that.
So, she walks in a world now where gods,
angels, and good parents are her last hope.

22 – A GOOD BAD KID

The sun burns bright at noon
when he opens the motel door
in nothing but his torn boxers
and yawns with both elbows
stretched up behind his head.

Austin's South by Southwest,
          part music festival...
          part eternity in hell,
is beginning to wind down
and the streets are full-awash
with humans all about his age
slowly destroying themselves
with alcohol and heroin, and
anything else they can score
while having a helluva time
as they do it, nonetheless.

Living forever's overrated.
So... he is doing his part
to avoid it.   And yet...

he had a long, vivid dream
in the night about his mom
sitting at the old kitchen table
back home, crying in the dark
with a cup of chamomile tea.

He woke up at one point...
but when he fell back asleep,
she was still there, still crying.

And he knows that getting
another barb-wire tattoo
won't cover up the way
he left things with her.

And he knows she did
what she had to to get him
into that exclusive arts school.

And he knows he's totally
fucking everything up.

And, he also knows
he's not quite done
doing that yet.

23 – A Change in Plans

His family's egregious wealth
expected much more from him.

You don't get a free ride through
the Tuck School of Business
at Dartmouth only to finish
in the middle of your class
with aspirations of being
a painter who focuses
on oils and acrylics
for God's holy sake.

Mom's trying to get him
to look at a bigger picture.
His father's not even talking.
An older brother laughs at him
with his colleagues over the long
conference table at Goldman Sachs.

And he understands… full well…
when he draws his index finger
along the prickle of hog bristle
on a favorite Sanden brush…

that they will never
feel this.

24 – HALF HER LIFE

As long as the music doesn't stop,
she doesn't have to think about it.

She's 24… and the music of not
thinking about it's been playing
for close to 12 of those years.

And over those 12 years,
the music's gotten darker,
the distorted guitars much,

much louder, and the voices
behind the guitars a lot darker,
louder… and much angrier…

because what she's trying not
to think about is getting much,
much harder not to think about…

because that one other more distant
voice—the one from 12 years ago—
is getting much darker… much
louder… and much angrier.

25 – BY THE TIME…

For those born to a small town,
the best chance to escape it is by
or even before the age of, say, 25.

After that point, you've had the job
at ACE Hardware, or the gas station,
long enough for expectations to set in.

By the late 30's, the dirt's in your bones
as bad as the floorboard of your truck,
and there is no gettin' that stuff out.

By the late 40's, you have forgotten
where the hell it was you were going
to run off or away to in the first place.

And by the late 50's, you begin to see
what it is that would've brought you
right back here someday if you had.

By the late 60's, you're buyin' a plot
down at the end of Cemetery Road.
And, truth is, you're pretty damned

satisfied with your view of eternity.

26 – EL MARTILLO

The pounding of his rusty
framing hammer beats out
the hard rhythm for his life.
A scarred pickaxe cracks at
the stones of his memories,
as well as hopes for a future.

So… why wouldn't he enjoy
waking that couple next door
from a slumber in paradise,
them and all the others who
stare at him from driveways,
shut windows and back doors.

Chingados… Americanos… who
live, laugh, and get it on under
the ceilings that he provides.
He's learned to ignore them,
though. Same way he ignores
the enough he will not be paid.

Pero, he works beneath *el cielo azul*.
And *los ojos* of his daughter will shine,
just as bright for him when he gets home.
So… it's on with pounding the rhythm,
the beat of a life that is not chosen…
but assigned by a thoughtless God.

27 – OF A CERTAIN KIND

She both loves,
it seems, and doesn't
love all of the attention.

There's a certain amount
at least… of a certain kind
she'd like to keep receiving.

Yet men seldom make those
same intricate distinctions.
(They seldom ever have.)

Or say, a certain amount
at least, of a certain kind
of men appear incapable.

She'll go on, though, and
continue to let them try—
and continue to try they will,

just as they will go on giving
attention, whether they ever
make the distinction or not.

Or, at least a certain amount
of a certain kind of attention,
the kind they've always given.

28 – ALL IN THE FAMILY

"Dad drove a tow truck too.
Took me with 'im one night
when I was, maybe, nineteen.

I-25 between Colorado Springs
and Pueblo—a couple of Toyota
4Runners'd hit head-on at 80 mph.

Anyway, both of 'em were like one,
now… and just about the size of…
I'd betya… your Camry back there.

One o' the guys they couldn't even
get out—so… we towed the three
or four pieces of 'im back with us

all the way to Jenkin's junk yard
in the middle of a cold night.
Can you believe that stuff?

Anyway I went into training
the next week, and I've been
drivin' a tow truck ever since."

29 – A Time to Embrace

29 years may have been enough
for her to realize that men are not
worth the stains they leave behind.

The surprise and the wet shudder
she had felt, long into last night…
while locked in the porcelain limbs

of a softer lover with obsidian hair
swaying, all the way down to those
dimples above the two most flawless

porcelain butt cheeks she'd ever had
the privilege of holding in her hands,
were enough to let her know that…

a tremendous change in the way
she's always done this particular
business… may be imminent.

30 – A No-show

For most of his 20s,
he'd felt that the age of 30
would be a kind of turning point.

But he never thought it might mean
a turning toward having absolutely
no idea what to do with himself
—let alone the rest of his life.

His childhood dream of being
a professional basketball player
was dashed when he maxed out
at five-foot-four in high school.

In college he enjoyed delusions
of *famous writer*, the short man's
best chance at getting a date—
but his early efforts made clear
he's really more the reader type.

After graduating with a bachelor's
in art history he thought he should
cut to the chase and go with ad copy,
or maybe investment banking—money
being a short man's second best chance.

But that plan lasted only seven weeks
into a course on statistics he took
in the first semester of an MBA

that lasted only a month or two
into the second semester of it.

And so… now? There is no way
he's showing up for Thanksgiving,
not with this amount of nothing
to offer his poor parents…

and the two big sisters
who both have nice
retirement packages.

31 – HE'S EVERY KIND

It took 31 years for him to realize
he's nothing more than that guy
who stuffs paper towels into
the urinal at the bar because
he's just an inebriated jackass.

And, his ex-wife made it clear
during the divorce proceedings
that with his mouth and temper,
he is also little more than a mean,
and sometimes terrifying, hardass.

And, since he failed Freshman Comp,
because he doesn't know where a damn
period goes in a sentence, he can't even
express this discovery he has just made,
because he's also too much of a dumbass.

32 – Unexpected

Condolences flood her phone
and Facebook page. She can't
keep up with the number…

let alone the varying degrees
of sincerity. So, surely everyone
will understand her reserved silence.

There are not, and have never been,
words for these kinds of absences.
And those who talk in spite of it

look like fish flopping on sand,
gasping for water… or some other
died-for thing that's only inches away.

    It was her mother…
       It was unexpected…
          The funeral is tomorrow…

And, she knows she has to keep it
to herself, that no one would ever
understand… how happy she is.

33 – You Got a Problem with It?

Blowing off his education
had become a political stance.

The Rebel Flag for a license plate…
his diploma for a degree in ignorance.

The barrel of his .45? Much more of
a big middle finger than a basic right.

Those dark clouds of exhaust billowing
from the diesel smokestacks on his F350?
Protests against the pansy-ass government
he refuses to actually know anything about.

And, if he's got an 18-inch Roman Cross
tattooed right in the middle of his back,
does it matter that he's never bothered
to read any one of the Four Gospels?

And is he wrong that too much learnin'
is just some other means of inbreeding?

And if y'ain't sure you heard him right,
he'd be happy to repeat what he's said,

just before he smashes a bottle o' Bud
across the side of your fucking skull.

34 – TOO LATE. OR NOT...

There will be all the 5-minute videos
to try to keep hidden from her kids,
which will be impossible... because
they'll have friends in seventh grade
who'll know all about those things.

There'll be the likely fading of
the relative understanding of
her current husband about
how much of it she had done.

And there will always be the loss
of her mother... who is alive...
living in Seattle with her father,
who is also forever lost to her.

There is a stretching that occurs
from overuse, not only in the skin,
but in the heart and the soul as well.
An unforeseen and exacting price
comes with the ecstatic abuse
of nature's most natural act.

But at 34 the phone's stopped
ringing—so, she's in the process
of enrolling in community college.
And, for the first time, she is...
truly thinking about change.

35 – THE LITTLE VOICE

Here on her 35th birthday,
her much younger self
is holding a come-to-Jesus
meeting with her current self.

> The younger self had hoped
> they'd have children by now.

In a huff, current self explains—
in too much detail—the feminism
they discovered during their Masters
in Social Justice makes clear the issues
of a world-strangling overpopulation?

> The younger shrugs her shoulders,
> says, "Whatever," with an eye-roll.
> "And, by the way, what is up sister
> with the two cats and pudgy belly."

"Now, hold on there, you little twit…
first of all, both of them are rescues,
and second, I feel no cultural need
to look photoshopped anymore.
And the sooner you get over
that bullshit, the better."

> "Ok… ease up. Geez…
> I'm just sayin'…"

"Yeah, that's right.
You *are* 'just sayin','
and you best back off
until you know what it is
you're talking about, bitch."

"A bit touchy, aren't we? Oh…
and don't think that I don't know
you are totally in love with that guy
who sits two cubicles over at work."

"Ok…
that is it!
Get out."

36 – Just Off Broadway

> "There is no poetry where there are no mistakes."
> ~ Joy Harjo

He's pulling into
the 19th town this month
with a guitar, a black shirt,
and a trunk full of new CDs.

He will stay at the nice house
of a beautiful woman married
to a nice man who's a huge fan.

It's just business as usual out here
on the road during touring season.

And the nice man'll chirp nervously,
and on and on, about his music,
especially this new album…
and about how awesome
the gypsy's life must be.

And the beautiful woman
will listen to them quietly…
while sliding an index finger
up and down the crystal stem
of a glass of very red wine.

And the nice man will
have always wanted

to do what he is doing.

And he'll smile, politely
reminding the nice man
of the pitfalls to the scene.

And they'll all get a little tipsy.

And the beautiful woman will
lightly touch his forearm when
she shows him the fresh linens.

And he's pretty sure she'll wish
she could sneak down the hall
sometime, later in the night.

And he's sure he wishes
she could do it too. But…
she won't… because of the
nice man she'll be in bed with.

And this little one-act play
will run again… about two
or three towns down the road.

And what doesn't quite happen
is a part of what makes
his life bearable.

37 – A Sad Dilemma

At 37, she's beginning to believe
the guy she's living with now
is an apology to her 20's—

the decade she spent seeking out
men, or boys, as they may have been,
who she felt deserved to be struck down.

And didn't they know it was coming?
After the way they'd treated other
girls in high school and college?

She'd had the looks, and special
skills, for the job and considered
herself a soldier in their sad cause.

More than all that, though, she had
a nut-job father and the hell of a past
to drive the whole thing over the cliff.

So now—now that she's still alive—
she's got this sweet young guy that
she doesn't want to hurt anymore,

but that she also does not love.

38 – LET IT SHINE

At her 20-year high school reunion,
she remembered the days, and well.

Her legs, as skinny as twin bedposts,
out on the cross-country running trail,
had been a matter of fun for the gum-
popping cheerleaders after practice.

Her hair, a dishwater blond ponytail,
didn't compare with the bad dye-jobs.
So, she focused on books and horses,
while they focused on what they could.

And now, two decades down the road,
through some perfecting force in nature,
muscle has blossomed all over her bones,
love has turned her skin to satin. And…
in her red silk dress, she simply radiates
an energy that burns beyond sexuality.

And the two cheerleaders who showed,
the others not having bothered, because
neither Jenny Craig nor the gastric sleeve
had gotten them down three sizes in time,
were keeping a closer eye on their husbands
than they were their glasses of Chardonnay,
while the husbands made meager attempts
to not make things ridiculously obvious.

39 – THESE KINDS OF THINGS

Recently released from seven years
in the dark cell and Stygian grip of
Borderline Personality Disorder—

the woman who loved to hate him
as much as she hated to love him—

he was no longer confident that love
was a thing he could feel anymore.

But, the woman before him now
is as kind as she is patient, calm
and un-needing of anything
that he can discern so far.

> And, yes… she is 61.
> And, yes… he is 39.

And though his very few friends
cock their heads from side to side
from time to time, everyone knows
there are no actual rules on the books
when it comes to the aim of Cupid.

But what he doesn't question
is how incredibly… almost
painfully… beautiful she is.

They had met at the reading
of an author they both enjoyed
in the Tattered Cover Book Store
on East Colfax Avenue in Denver.

And though his heart is still sulking
like a teenager in a broken family,
he is old enough to know this:

that a bonding over books
is not a thing to take lightly.

40 – AN INVISIBLE MAN

The hats and thick scarves,
sunglasses and stubbly beard,
do not cover his biggest regret.

After all the Grammy nominations,
the three wins, even that one Oscar,
he still cannot have the thing he wants.

His supermodel wife, who the *Enquirer*
claims is cheating with a Saudi prince,
doesn't do much to help him either.

No limousine can whisk him off
or far enough away—no number
of bodyguards can clear the space.

No nine-foot fence in Beverly Hills,
no lawsuit filed against the paparazzi,
not even some social media death hoax.

None of it can give him back the one
thing he craves more than life itself,
since he doesn't have a life anymore.

His one last ambition: to walk the streets
at noon, order a triple caramel Frappuccino,
maybe buy a can of those Vienna Sausages

down at the gas station on the corner,
then savor them slowly on a bench
over in Echo Park—and *not*

have a picture of it show up
on the opening montage
of the next damnable

installment of—
*Entertainment
Tonight.*

41 – When to Fold 'Em

She noticed that his panic
over who would get what
had taken a step toward
menacing in recent days,

and that it was less about
what he wanted and more
what he needed to make
sure she would not get.

The game was knocking
at the door of so-obvious
by this point, she decided
to shift her entire strategy.

So she asked him, finally,
if she could, maybe, keep
her underwear and socks.
"Underwear," he asked?

Yes. And maybe enough
shirts and pants to get her
wherever she was going.
And… that was that…

It'd worked like a hunter
draining the buck's blood
after the kill… in order
to preserve the meat.

And as she drove off,
the eyes in the back of
her head saw the whole
scene play like a movie—

every book, every plate...
every cup, saucer, couch...
every dresser and spatula...
all the pictures in frames...

becoming concrete suitcases
that, for the rest of his sad life,
he would never quite be able
to fit in his pathetic trunk.

42 – A Dark Decision

Through the sharp lens of his 5-25x
sniper scope, scenes had played out
and the things had gone down—

just like they had in the movies
his dad took him to growing up.

Orders came through, he pulled
the trigger. The system made
a kind of surrealistic sense.

But now, at 42, his retirement,
for reasons he won't talk about,
is boring the shit out of him…

and he's got somebody willing
to pay him a hell of a lot more
than the military did in a year

for a single job.

43 – PROBABLY SOONER

She loves him. She's sure.
He loves her. She knows.

But, not to the extent
that he'll leave his wife,
whom he loves more…
and she knows that too.

So she maintains a certain
dignity in her occasional
interactions with both.

Because she loves her too,
as strange as that may seem.

She's not a terrible person.
And she has known her
a lot longer. But still…

a rending has occurred
in the hem of the universe,

and so… sooner or later,
something will unravel.

44 – MAYBE LATER

He continued the game, so he said,
well past wanting to play it anymore,
with the women who kept believing
that he'd kept believing somehow
a single word he'd ever sung, so
they just kept coming, coming
to his shows to hear the words
he'd long stopped believing, yet
words he just kept singing now,
never moving, his eyes always
closing, except when pausing
to lift the next complimentary
shot to his lips, the lips they
kept watching and wanting
to lock onto with theirs,
in some kind of believing
that the sound of their coming
later that night would somehow
have some kind of meaning.

45 – It All Goes Back

At 45, he doesn't know
how he went from a relentless
love for good books in his early 20's

to the professor who wants to make sure
everything's done unto his grad students
that was done unto him, back when
he stood in their struggling shoes.

He takes a preternatural joy almost,
in making sure the code is followed.

Even to the point that he wonders
if his professors could've actually
done that amount of damage...

and that maybe it all goes back
to a father who worked long days
on an assembly line, then came home
at night to drink cheap beer, and to ask
his son—at the top of his smoky lungs—

if those goddam books were ever gonna
help him get a life, for God's sake.
Maybe even a goddam job.

46 – GOODBYE TO HOLLYWOOD

One huge movie
was enough to do it.
A big role in his teens,
and that was it... all over.
A child star, but not a child.
Not good, just severely cute,
and funny, as an actor playing
that one character the one time.

So, the second attempt bombed
when the funny just couldn't hide
the not good part. And soon after,
cocaine erased all of the cuteness...
and, as I said... that was it... all over.
So now, he haunts the streets of Taos
in a tweed beret, grumbling to himself
at the Laundromat by Smith's grocery.

Nobody knows where, not for sure,
the little bit of money comes from,
when, or how, they get it to him,
whoever "they" happen to be.
But, he gets it, and uses it,
to buy pot, rolling blunts
as bribes to young hippies
for necklaces and hand jobs.

And that's it...   all over.

47 – O Lord

Lord, have mercy...
the poor, lost souls
all over the world...
so many to pray for,
and she does it every
morning... every noon...
and every God-given night.

Lord, help her...
she just can't sleep
for the anguish she feels
for all those who will never
know the joy and holy peace
of a life lived safely locked
in the Everlasting Arms.

Lord, Jesus Christ...
she will never rest until
you return to deliver Love
to all who have set their lives
on cruise control... their souls
careening down that dark road
to Satan's infernal living room.

O Lord, and Personal Savior...
heed her weary, long-suffering
laments for the Devil's minions
who revel in their gluttonous ways
and rejoice in too much fermentation

of the fruits of thy creation,
chiefly… crushed grapes.

Lord, God of Heaven…
smite the forces of evil, and
the followers of foreign gods,
in order to rain down your holy
grace upon the nations, covering
all the earth in a big divine blanket
of your goodness and blessings.

And dear, sweet Jesus…
please bring her only son
back into the heavenly fold…
save him from the temptations
of his education in liberal arts…
and, that vile young woman who
sneaks into his dorm room at night.

God of the saints, have mercy…
on her tirelessly devoted heart,
the heart she has sacrificed
on a blood-stained altar
of services rendered
in the Great Cause—
the promise of salvation.

48 – NOT EVEN 50 YET

That damned right elbow
has caused him problems
for almost a year it seems,
and still isn't up to speed.

And now, the left elbow
is in the same sad shape
from compensating for
the damned right elbow.

He upped the glucosamine
from 500 to 800 milligrams,
takes his turmeric religiously.
That's helped his fingers a bit.

But, both of his damned knees
are down to bone on bone now,
and his lower back is totally shot
from the days of track and soccer,

echoes of old news he re-receives
every time he has to bend down
to pick up the morning's paper.
Going to hell is a slow process.

But when the right elbow went,
just trying to slide on and Velcro
the brace on his left? He knew…
he was nearing the Gates of Hell.

49 – THE MISSED WINDOW

At 49, he feels he's now passed
the window, missed his chance
to live two separate lives across
the border of two separate states,

to sleep with two separate wives
in two different beds, one wife
in the one state, and another one
in the other, neither known to either,

with enough shelves between the two
places to hold all his books, the best
of his acoustic guitars in its case here,
and his favorite electric on a stand there,

maybe even a set of sisters and brothers
who never meet their half-sisters or
half-brothers, a poodle for one set,
and a couple of cats for the others,

and maybe even the complicated days
would be worth the mileage and effort.
Or, maybe not.   Either way,
he feels he's passed the window now.

50 – DIAGNOSIS: NOT I, SAID HE

He considers 50 years to be
about 25 too many for him
to have finally figured this out.

The first person pronoun is not
the problem in confessional
writing. It is narcissism—

as a basic philosophical
belief, we could say—
that does most of us in.

And it is not a question of
whether one has it, or doesn't,
but the extent to which each does,

as well as how far the curved line
representing the poets in our chart
goes beyond the finite edge of the page.

Still... it's good to know the source
of this all too common sickness,
so he can finally seek its cure.

51 – MIDLIFE CHRISTMAS

That 51st
Christmas Morning
came on a mouse's toes,

the sound of the brown
extension cord's head
sliding into the socket,

lighting up the fir tree
to the sound of a kettle
roiling up to a boiling,

an early hour alone,
before the soft waking,
and then the sole-stirring,

his lover's yawning smile
on the pad of pink slippers
that brings a white-pajama kiss.

52 – WHAT IT IS

Once you've made it
to the top of Canyon Road,
Santa Fe's all downhill from there.
Though… she stopped romancing
the whole adobe scene years ago.

She grabbed coffee and a bagel
from Café Des Artistes and
headed up the sidewalk.

Just past Garcia Street,
she saw a Yorky terrier
in a red sweater and little
red rubbery hiking booties
lift up its hind leg at the base
of a bronze sculpture in the yard
of the VENTaNa Fine Art studio.

Further up, a band of French students
were trying on a Texas accent for size
while taking pictures of each other as
they mimicked an installation piece.

And, she's aware the restaurants
are overpriced. And she knows
a lot of the art is questionable
at best. But… right now…

her work is selling well. And,
she does love this mad place
with almost a sort of pain
down deep in her heart.

And Santa Fe, in a way,
may be mostly a depiction
of what it once was, as well
as what it ever hoped to be.

But… she's not leaving.

53 – A BIG MOVE

It's his last chance, at 53,
to make the big, final move.

The third of three just headed out
for Trinity U. down in San Antonio.
The company's getting ready for yet
another shakedown in personnel.
His wife hasn't spoken to him,
really, in over a decade now.

So, before the end of summer,
he'll clean out the secret account,
hit 281 North up to Devil's Lake
in the last of the Dakotas… then
throw his phone out the window
when he crosses Canada's border
and turns west onto Highway 2
into Southern Saskatchewan…

where the log cabin he bought
from some business colleague
last year awaits him there…
somewhere by the shores
of the Moose Jaw River.

54 – ALL OF IT

She'd never imagined
there might come the day
when she couldn't call him
on all his bullshit anymore.

The next day's promise of
yet another opportunity
had always been there,
with its solid guarantee.

But, last night he tossed
his muddy boots, empty
beer cooler, and all his
dirty socks and boxers

in the back of his truck,
along with all his bullshit,
and he hasn't answered one
of her eighteen or more calls.

And now, she just wants him...
the dirty socks and muddy boots,
even the beer cooler and boxers,
along with all his bullshit... back.

55 – NO MORE

55 years of keeping mom and dad
away from each other's throats.

55 years of talking all her sisters
and brothers out of running away,
since they were younger. And now,
into coming home for the holidays.

55 years of apologizing, once again,
to concerned neighbors next door.

55 years of gathering up her mom's
lowball glasses and rinsing them out,

as well as 55 years of her dad cursing her
for not leaving those glasses where they fell
and letting her mother deal with her own mess.

But mostly… 55 years of believing
it was, somehow, her fault.

56 – The Situation Room

The young yoga ladies invade
the coffee shop on the square
after their 10:00 a.m. session.
So, she makes sure to speak
over their annoying chatter
a little more forcefully to her
friend who's feigning interest.

She's upset because the interior
decorator is attempting to go with
the smaller trim around the vanity
in the bathroom, and he's being
quite overbearing about it all.
The wallpaper he's selected
is atrocious, and she wants
the bigger trim to cover up
as much of it as possible—
"Understandable," of course,
her quiet friend finally concedes.

Anyway the whole affair is simply
wearing her out. She's just dying
for this to be over and done with,
for heaven's sake. And she knows,
without any doubt, when she gets
the sink situation ironed out…
she'll have some peace in life.

57 – CERTAIN

At 57, he stares just over the rim
of his third glass of Tempranillo,
a bit shell-shocked that he is alive.

He doesn't remember what the plan
had been—or whether there'd even
been a plan to begin with… but…

it's far too late for a new one now.
And his rheumatic fingers missed
certain notes, on certain strings,

in the show last night, the show
where a few certain women still
gave him a certain look when

he played certain songs, but
that look is getting as old as
their faces are tired n' drawn.

There is no IRA, however…
so… there'll be no retirement.
Which means, come morning,

he'll get up and pack his gear
in the van again… then go
pick up the boys in town.

58 – Restraint

He arrived to the 1960s
sometime in the mid 70s,
and was late to everything
else for the rest of his life.

He'd gone to a small Baptist
university, because the drugs
were better and being a hippie
was still, somewhat, exotic.

But when the last of many
nailed him to a set of vows,
and in came that first child,
out went the guitars, the tie-
dye t-shirts, a Godspell fro.

From there, he went slowly
and carefully insane… since…
up to that point he'd been faking.

He's worked (in some strange way)
for the government through a string
of decades, and four more children,
whom he loves dearly and devotedly.

And now, at 58, he's alone for a bit
on his back porch, feet propped up
to a sunset and a glass of red wine,

and realizing, for the first time,
he's accomplished at least one
astonishing feat in his life—

He is a serial killer
who never acted
on the impulse.

59 – Getting Older

Today, there will be
no diagnosis because,
frankly, you've sensed
no need to see a doctor
in well over a year or two.

Today, the car will not flip
on the return from the bar
back to the house because,
the roads aren't all that slick,
you live in a very small town,
and you plan on driving safely.

Tonight, you'll sip a margarita
or two, along with leftover
mushroom and spinach
quesadillas because,
they are really good
and, to tell the truth,
you drink a margarita
or two almost every night.

So, in a minute or two, maybe,
step outside and look to the sky
that has mostly cleared up now,
breathe deeply and offer thanks
for the days when nothing much
happens, and the news—as long

as you don't turn on a television—
has to do with neighbors talking
at the ends of driveways about
fawning season, the rebuilding
after all the recent floods, and
the dogs breaking out today.

Real trouble will return,
someday. But...
why be in
a hurry
for it.

He views it as responsible hoarding.
The piles sing to him as he walks
through the aisles they create.

Newspapers and magazines,
shot glasses, Zippo lighters.
That's hoarding. Old clothes,
snow globes, pocket knives.

But no… not good books.
No… a house full of books
has not to do with hoarding.
This needs a different name.

And maybe it *is* hoarding.
But these pages are friends,
people he's known for decades.
Some of them real characters too.

And their voices are the Voices
of the Ages… mouths filled
with the great words of this
and every time that's passed.

If a great thought was thought,
it was likely thought of between
these hard and paperback covers.

These books, with their stories
that comfort him every night
he spends alone in his bed
surrounded, of course,
by even more books,
are his soulmates.

So, if you want
to call it hoarding,
then call it hoarding.

What does he care?

61 - UNCOMFORTABLE

After her husband started working
days *and* nights with that new
secretary, fifteen years ago,

she'd taken up with novels
and decided they served just
as well for a love relationship.

That's why, when she attended
the reading by a favorite author
at the Tattered Cover Bookstore,

the young man who took the seat
right next to her did not register
with her senses—at least until...

they turned to look at each other
while chuckling about some scene
from the beginning of Chapter 1.

But after a question or two here
and an admission or two there
while in line for the signing...

she began to feel uncomfortable,
and in a way that made her desire
to be made more uncomfortable.

So, they met for coffee there
at the bookstore the next week,
which made her uncomfortable.

Coffee she did not want to drink,
because she never does. But coffee
she drank anyway, because… well…

she was so pleasantly uncomfortable.
Coffee she decided she might enjoy
after all. And coffee she choked on

when she found out that he was 39.
And, if that made her a little more
uncomfortable… all of a sudden…

she was just as surprised to see how
quickly her concern began to fade.
So what if that meant 22 years…

So what if she'd lost her ability
to gauge the physical age of
a mature, and literate, man.

And so what if none of her friends,
or anyone else she happens to know,
is going to believe…   this one.

62 – On the Range

You're born where you're born,
where your parents make a living.
Your choices are between Ford or
Chevy, John Deere or Ditch Witch,

or which of the only three flavors
of ice cream to buy down at Aunt
Betty Jo's store: vanilla, chocolate,
or the strawberry. And so it is...

that God gave him a home
where the buffalo roam
and graze the prairie grass
down to nothin' but stubble,

and the deer and the antelope
play, and mate, and devour
everything in sight, then shit
all over God's good creation,

where seldom is heard
a discouraging word—
　　or an encouraging one,
　　　　come to think of it...

and the skies are not cloudy
all day, because the drought
is goin' on six years now and
the crops are dyin' in the fields.

63 – BORE-SIZE AND GAUGE

At 63, his few remaining friends
just weren't enough in number
to buffer him from all the folks
he'd pissed off in this Texas town,

here where no resident's a stranger
and no stranger's all that welcome
to try and convert into a resident.

So, he's looking for some land
in the far west corner of this
big-ass state so full o' big-ass
hats and big-ass pickup trucks,

not to mention all its crazy-ass
unspoken laws and protocols,

crazy-ass rules written down
in no particular record book
by no particular fat politician,

but rules enforced nonetheless
by every caliber and bore-size,
every gauge of gun that exists.

64 – STILL RIVER

Her mind and body
decided to part ways
after a long, loving,
and beautiful affair.

Her body has begun
to embrace the one law
of inertia, that an object
at rest tends to stay at rest,
and has squatted in the dirt,
refusing to go any further
in life's tiresome journey.

Her mind, however,
has turned around,
turned backward,
and is retracing
the thousand miles
toward her childhood
home… to a still river
near there, where she is
determined to learn again
how to skip smooth stones
across the still surface,
while sauntering
up and down
the bank.

65 – PILING UP

His life was a disorganized stack
of his half-thought-out reasons
for never quite getting around
to anything that truly matters.

He'd piled them in the farthest
corner of his Hooker oak desk
that he only has a day or two
to clean out for the new guy.

65 years had gone by faster
than the cliché that forever
warns us how time flies—
until our time has flown.

So, as he loads the last
couple of boxes, he has
absolutely no idea where
to put the stack of reasons.

66 – Driven

The big-rigs had been
her ticket out of, and far away
from, the Fort Apache Reservation,
back when she thought she would die
if she didn't leave. And in the days
of her early 20s… that might,
very well, have been true.

For over 40 years, she's driven
18-wheelers along sparse patches
of I-40—from Flagstaff, Arizona
to Greensboro, North Carolina
and back again—and now…
they're telling her to retire.

But, she's done it so long,
she just doesn't know what
"one place" means anymore.

She's burned so many miles,
she feels partly responsible
for the rotation of the earth.

She's traveled so far for so long,
and passed so many exits now,
it would take every damn one
of those 40 years over again
to get back to Fort Apache.

67 – BECAUSE HE'S DEAD

It's never too late
to be too late
to honor a man
for his good work

and therefore decide
to honor a man anyway
at the awards ceremony
where it is now too late
to give him the award…

so you give it to his widow
who is quite aware that it is
too late to offer this award
but, she steps up anyway
to honor him with a few
reluctantly chosen words
that will never be as good
as his words had been…

                which is why
everyone's here tonight
in order to honor him
with this award…

that comes…
too late.

68 - FLAT

She dreams of a level world.

Despite the theories of Pythagoras,
   or Magellan's so-called "proof,"

she would thoroughly prefer that all
the earth's holes be thoroughly filled
and raked smooth by an unseen crew,

while every lump and mound is cleanly
shaved back down to its original state.

The place is an extraordinary mess…
something must be done. And, she is
completely appalled… not to mention
worn out by the fact that she is the one
having to do all of the worrying about it.

69 – Broadcasting

At 69, he still feels the flat fedora
with that red feather in the band
is working the way it always had,

especially with the 2-inch ponytail
poking out below the black felt rim,

a gray period under some exclamation
that was missing the desired point—

mainly because the Grateful Dead
t-shirt and cargo shorts hovering
above white socks in Birkenstocks
says so much more… which is…

that he ran sound for the band
back in the 70's, as opposed to
played lead guitar… which is…

the message that he still believes
the black fedora and gray ponytail
are sending out into the coffee shop.

70 – FORWARD TO THE PAST

So, she moved to Santa Fe
because LSD and mushrooms
made more sense than iPhones.

And she moved out here by herself
because none of the men she loved
had survived the late 1960s in tact.

And she remembers a few bad trips
of her own, but nothing as scary as
Bob Dylan's new Christmas album.

So, at 70, she got rid of everything
but the cat, and the car to put it in,
and drove to the Sangre de Cristos.

It wasn't soon enough to do this…
but it wasn't too late either. And now
that she's here, the smell of piñon fires,

all the indecipherable art on Canyon Road,
and the odd way people dress in this town,
just make her feel something like 19 again.

71 – CALL BACK

It had been the plan all along,
he said with a mud-caked boot
propped on the back bumper
of an old rusting Ford F250.

Sure, he took off for a while.
Every son and daughter does
who grows up in the panhandle.
Even the good sons n' daughters.

He'd served in one of the wars.
But, younger folks these days
don't really care which it was.
He doesn't care that they don't.

He got a degree at Massachusetts
Institute of Technology. Nuclear
physics. Used it for a while...
down south of Houston.

Spent some time in Geneva too,
but, like he said, this was the plan.
Granddaddy's ten thousand acres
right here, in Cimarron County.

Yep... when Oklahoma calls
a boy back home, no matter
how far away you might be,
you go ahead and pack up.

72 – SILENCE EVERYONE

The world has gotten
too loud for her now…

> those big screen TVs
> and the praise band over
> at the Presbyterian church…
> the Gas Station Network when
> she fills up the car at Walmart…
> and, she'll never again step foot
> into a movie theater… ever…

The overhead traffic in and out
of their regional airport nearby
has tripled in the last ten years.

The neighbor behind her is new
and younger… and she can feel
the bass from his huge speakers
in the floorboards of her house.

The girl standing in front of her
in line at the grocery store today
played a YouTube video with all
the volume a phone has to offer.

And so she's afraid she may soon
be forced to shut her front door
and just never go outside again.

73 – THUMB-TWIDDLING

So much time on his hands.
He doesn't know what to do
with all these hours that pile up
like unanswered letters thrown on
to a desk where he no longer works.

Self improvement seems responsible.
He watches TEDTalks on PBS some.
He likes to listen to NPR in the truck
when he decides to go buy avocados,
or ice cream, for no particular reason.

The other day he heard that the cells
in our DNA have little off-switches.
And that after a certain amount of
strictly designated time, they just
flip down. That's it… all done.

This morning he caught himself
staring at his half-rotten avocados
sitting in a bowl on the kitchen table,
and imagining a billion tiny light bulbs
going out, one by one, inside his body.

74 – How It's Done

Of course the morning coffee
must be slow-poured, by hand,
from the steel stove-top kettle,
and through a single-cup cone.

The bread, that goes with it,
should be toasted, but lightly,
and on one side—then spread
with room-temperature butter
and, absolutely, apricot jelly.

She cooks one egg, as long as
it's from her hairdresser's hens.
She likes it sunny-side-up—but
pokes the yoke, so it runs along
the top and into the skillet a bit.
That allows for even cooking,
as common sense demands.

She arranges a plate and cup
at the setting, to the left side
of the kitchen table. The sun
is altogether too bright over
there on the right, you see.

It is always a bite of toast
followed by a sip of coffee,
for the best mingling of flavors.

And always after the turn of each
page of the morning's newspaper,
that she reads from back to front,
because she likes a strong ending.

And... she does not know what
everyone is whispering about...
when her kids and grandkids visit.
The rule is clear and easy to follow:

The morning schedule will continue
as planned, down to every detail...
and she is not to be disturbed until
she is done with the day's headline.

75 – BAD FORM

Even after 75 years
of incessant practice,

his stories continued
to make the mistake

of telling us, detail
after excruciating

detail, precisely,
and o n l y …

what happened.

76 – Two's Enough

There used to be ways to take care
of all kinds of domestic problems.

When old folks caught this or that
disease, they'd just up and die of it.

When young men did certain things
to young women, they paid for it,
usually in a manner appropriate
to whatever he'd gone and done.

Now'days there're so many damn
laws on the books you can't even
tell someone what you're thinkin'
about doin' with your problems.

But… the doctors have told him
they can't stop the tumor this time.
And… everybody in town knows
what the Thompson boy'd done
to his precious granddaughter.
And he knows damn well where
the Thompson boy lives, son'bitch.

So, that's why… when he steps out
of the woodshed in the backyard…
there'll be one shell in the barrel,
and a second one in his pocket.

77 – Sure Enough

It had been some 20 to 30 years
since she'd climbed on the thing.

Her hippie-chick daughter used it,
liked it for running errands in town
when she visited from Los Angeles.

But the daughter was not there today.
The sun is out. Hers was a quiet street.
And she didn't know why she couldn't.

So she rolled it out onto the driveway,
put her right foot on the right pedal,
considered for a second what could
go wrong, and then… shoved off.

> The wheels whirled…
> the sprockets swirled…
> the air pulled at her hair.

And she was shocked
to find out that…

it is, indeed,
just… like…
riding a bicycle.

When he meets his longtime friends
at the diner on Monday mornings,
he keeps quiet on certain topics.
Like how weirdly old they look.
Or like, how sadly old they act.
He wants to slap 'em at times
and tell them to get a grip—
holler things like, "C'mon!
We are *not* done yet, guys!"

But he cannot explain to them
what he can't explain to himself.
That he still wants life to feel like
a James Dean movie… wants to go
back to "East of Eden" on a big silver
screen, back to "Rebel Without a Cause."
He has good years left, and he is not going
to spend them waiting for death over coffee.

And dammit by next Monday he's gonna finish
his restoration of that '55 Bel Air convertible.
That, or he'll damn well die trying. Then…
he will screech up in front of this place
and yell, "Who's in?" at the window.

He'll give 'em to the count of 10,
raising one finger at a time…
then burn some rubber.

79 – PAIN THRESHOLD

Who wouldn't mourn
the loss of a real bone?

Titanium has no marrow.

So, this has been as much
an amputation of the soul
as it has been the calcium
and cartilage in the knee.

What's missing in her now
hurts her more than the pain
in the process of replacement.

Learning to walk again feels
like living a lie. Every step,
a brutal step away from
God's original intent.

Therefore, please,
don't talk to her
about signs of
improvement.

80 – Take All These, and Call in the Morning

A few steps into his 80's now,
he works the lever of the blue

plastic pill cutter like a veteran
at position on an assembly line.

Almost as if there is a little flare
to some of the motions it seems.

Six in the morning, three at lunch,
another four or five with his dinner.

One for the heart, two for the diabetes,
three for blood pressure, and four to go.

When the day comes, down the road,
there will be no way to know which

condition finally took him down, but
she's so glad he's still here with us now.

So, she helps him count all of them out,
cries sometimes when he's not looking.

Two hearts that will not separate
as easily as all those pills.

81 – YET ANOTHER

After 53 good years of
a highly contentious
and yet, somehow,
loving marriage,
he ups and dies.

Just one more
confounded thing
for her to get upset
with and about over.

She wanted to tell him…
now that only one or maybe
two of the things she had ever
fought him on had really been
worth all of their troubles…

and as for all the rest of it,
she is, genuinely, sorry.

Though… the shock
of such an admission
would've been enough
to kill him all over again.

82 – ONE

His daughter drove away,
leaving him with just one car.

Dinner tonight will be Chinese
takeout with one place-setting.

The bed has two worn pillows,
but he's only going to need one.

Come morning, he'll fry one egg
to go with his one piece of toast.

And before long he won't be able
to take one, more, day of all this.

83 – THE BAKER

At 83 the old cast-iron kettle
she bakes leavened bread in
aggravates her arthritic fingers
when she pulls it from the oven.

Some combination of sheer will
and muscle-memory is the only
way she is still able to do it—
along with many other things.

Bread has been in our DNA
for ten thousand years longer
than science has been trying
to figure out exactly why.

And, what the smell of it
does to us has never needed
any kind of explanation—or
a detailed instruction manual.

She defies the Hitlers and Huns
of all generations with her one
simple skill—the very maker
and sustainer of all history.

84 – WHO'S TO JUDGE

He remembers most
the bologna sandwiches
they would stop and make
along the side of Route 66,

one slice each, for mom, dad,
and his five brothers and sisters.
Usually with onion... sometimes
tomato, but always on white bread.

They made the trip many times
from southwestern Oklahoma
to California's Central Valley,
following the Dust Bowl trail,

the ones who'd stayed following
those who'd left the dark clouds,
to celebrate the family reunions
up in Yosemite National Park

during the late 30s and through
the early 1940s in their old Ford
Roadking sedan with a V8 engine,
and he doesn't recall a bad memory.

The Grand Canyon. And that huge
meteor crater outside of Winslow.
He remembers his dad could not
get over the Petrified Forest...

that trees could turn to rocks.
"Yeah… we were as poor as
the red dirt we called home.
But we just didn't know it."

85 – WHO?

All the names of those she loves most
are, one by one, walking away from her
like characters at the end of a movie
in which things did not work out.

Remember—think for God's sake.
But… she's beginning forget as well
what remembering was to begin with.

The doctor is talking about arteries,
some condition, with a long name,
but she can't remember that either.

And, if our hands weaken in grip
over time, wouldn't our minds
just do the same, eventually?
That makes as much sense
as anything else anymore.

But it hurts in an awful way
to hear this woman standing
before her now tell her she
is her daughter, and yet
simply not be able
to remember
her name.

86 – THE SECOND CUP

63 years together,
and every morning
he makes the tea while
she butters toasted bread.

They sit in comfy chairs
with worn cotton throws
covering up shins and toes,
and play an old CD of hymns
on the portable home stereo
given to them by grandkids
on a Christmas long ago.

After their second cup,
he lines up his orange
prescription bottles...
while she scrambles up
three eggs, always three.
And then they fuss over
who should get more egg.

And this is more than symbiosis...
they're a masterpiece of architecture,

proof of a love that almost
surpasses God's.

He'd gotten old,
for lack of contact…
until the new neighbors
moved in next door to him.

A sad but lovely young woman
with a sad and lovely daughter
with two long, golden braids.

He baked a loaf of rye bread,
an odd thing he still liked to do,
and took it over, mostly because
of their sadness that he couldn't
keep from suffering himself…

and the inexplicable friendship
had been immediate, as happens
sometimes when friendships
are arranged by the angels.

A friendship that arose
from the ashes of two
different desperations,
one being the residue of
coming home to a husband
inside another woman on top
of their new stylish kitchen table,

the other leftover from
the recent and terrible loss
of, as good as love ever gets.

And over the weeks and months
all three of their faces, slowly,
learned to form smiles again.

And, though he can't speak
for them, the young woman's
hugs, when she brings over extra
groceries that she somehow knows
he needs, and the daughter's endless
queries that stream out when she wraps
her arms up around her knees, sitting
on the steps of his warped porch...

feel, a little, like going back to
the church he never wanted
to enter again... after God
had taken away from him
the world's best example
of heaven's holy love.

88 – MAKING PEACE

She's here at the Methodist church
this morning, in her Easter-best,
because the idea of a dead son
coming back to life is a thing
she still wants to believe in.

But she no longer bears
the illusion that, when
it comes to raising boys,
God is the best of fathers.

No. She comes for the sons.
The ones who die on the cross
for the Lord's lack of a better plan.

And she holds no bitterness over hers.
Not for the Father, nor for the plan.

She just knows now
that even God
has his flaws.

89 – ON THE ROCKS

She came home from Doris's funeral
yesterday afternoon and, now, cannot
bring herself to do anything responsible.

Doris had been her best friend for 80
of their 89 years, the one who knew
everything about her. Everything...

the one whose lap she'd collapsed in
when she lost her first son to cancer
and then, recently, her belovéd Walt.

So, it seemed she'd been responsible
long enough. She's just tired of being
the one who has got to stay behind.

Besides, who's left to care if she did
take that expensive bottle of Scotch
down from the mantle—where Walt

had always kept it for no good reason,
except to embarrass her every time
their pastor came by for a visit—

something she suddenly realized...
over that ninth, or maybe tenth sip...
she'd always loved about that old rascal.

90 – HANDS AND FINGERS

Not vanity… but
a certain grace, poise,
had always been her way
of moving through her life.

And yet, a mother's hands
are required to be a matter
of function, not decoration.

These fingers have lived long
and worked hard, and so they
look like the old crooked roots
of a great oak tree spreading out
to hold the earth's crust together.

Fingers that peeled and applied
over 500 Band-Aids… cooked
over 30,000 meals… and cut
the circulation of blood, one
from the other, while clenched
in the throes of countless prayers
for the sakes of those she raised
and released out into the world.

Prayers that bent them aslant
at the knuckles… wrung them
full of wrinkles… and left them
pale from wiping tears in dimly lit
hours she's kept mostly to herself.

Hours she keeps to herself now
because she doesn't want anyone
to see these old hands and fingers.

Hands and fingers that've become
a sacred work of art, nonetheless,
to the well-trained eye of God.

A God who has yet
        to convince her
her hands and fingers
        are beautiful.

91 – WHY BOTHER

The doctor told him decades ago
he needed to quit the daily scotch
with a cigar. They were both bound
to kill him... in two different ways.

Down the road from that advice,
the same doctor suggested that
caffeine was the worst culprit
in his sporadic bouts of reflux.
He'd said thanks and ignored it.

After that doctor died, the new
younger one expressed concern
over the recent marijuana habit,
which, honestly, is no such thing.
He just likes a little hit of the stuff
now and then, since his son-in-law
had introduced him to it during
the cancer treatments about
twenty-five years back or so.
Geez... has it been that long?

Anyway, both doctors are dead now.

92 – THE LORD'S SUPPER

On the quarterly Sunday mornings
when the church she used to attend
holds communion, she goes back
to her sitting room and draws
the velvet curtains to a seal.

She tunes into the service
on a transistor radio, pours
a crystal cordial of Lambrusco,
about half full, and sets it beside
a slice of her homemade bread.

She dims the lamp. She lights
a few choice candles—gifts
from that daughter-in-law
she loves as much as the son.

She waits, in this near darkness,
for the pastor's cues, followed by
the soft piano music, played by
the old hands of an old friend.

And it is, once again, the bread
and wine… the body and blood.
And if Jesus were to return today,
he would tiptoe past the back doors
of the church, and come straight here.

93 – ANOTHER WEDNESDAY

A 93rd birthday
on yet another Wednesday
in his life. So many Wednesdays
in his life, who could count anymore?

But, he had always enjoyed Wednesdays
just fine. Not everyone does, you know.
What he'd loved, though, was coffee.
For goin' on 75 years now anyway.

A couple of cups a day, at least.
Wow, how many would that be?
And, for those same 75 years…
he has been in love with her…

though she moved on to a place
he was not allowed to follow—
9 years and almost 2 months ago,
God rest his soul, as well as hers.

But, the kids will be here today.
Minus one. Lost him in the war.
Maybe a few grandkids'll come,
in lieu of the friends he misses.

So on the whole, he'd say,
not a bad Wednesday.

94 – LORD, NO... AND YES

Fear death?
Lord, no.

After 94 long years now
of working the fields of earth,
the lily-filled meadows of heaven
will be a more than welcome sight.

She rubs her numb right hand
and turns a stiff, short neck
to peer out a wind-rattled
pane of thin, blotchy glass.

Grateful though?
Lord, yes.

And for every last minute
of her plain and simple life.
Like a plain and simple flower...

it can be just as beautiful as any other,
if you're among those who actually stop,
look into its face, and really lean in
to smell its sweet perfume.

Sad to go?
Lord, no.

She pats her left knee
and taps a worn-out cane
on the dusty wooden planks
of her kitchen floor that oozes
the aroma of chicken she's fried
for longer than many people live.

Won't miss the pain,
nor that grease.

Ready then?
Lord, yes.

95 – THE IMPRESSIONIST

~ for N. L. B.

She remembers a master's in art,
somewhere back before three sons.

She'd put away the brushes for them.
Something she would not do again...
learning late that boys raise themselves.

When the third graduated high school,
the brushes came back out. And now,
    after five decades of workshops,
    festivals, blue ribbons, and galleries
    from Santa Fe to Carmel, California,
her studio's a living sea of oil and acrylic.

And, by 95, she has made the world
more beautiful than it actually is.

And she's done it by steering clear
of hard edges and well-defined lines.

And with every new day, she still hopes
the next will be better than the last.

And every day, it seems to be...
in spite of a hand that shakes
a little more each time she tries
to dip into some shade of Naples
yellow that she has just mixed...

and in spite of her eyes that strain
a bit harder each time she steps up
to a new canvas with the bristles
dripping that alizarin crimson.

Though the edges get
softer over time...
those lines even
less defined...

her impression
of God's world
will never fade.

She is by no means
obsessed with death.
She just never thought
she'd have so much time
to think about it. My God.

Her frail bones have ached
for so many decades now…
she no longer feels the pain.
Or… she doesn't notice it.

Long life has less to do with
what we're able to endure
and more what we can
get acclimated to. Or,
maybe she means what
we can fool ourselves
into believing over time.

Anyway, being 96 isn't near
as scary as she thought it'd be
back when she was, say, 56.

And… just between her
and her 40-years-ago self,
she loved as much as ever
watching that sun rise,
again, this morning.

97 – In 2016

He'd voted in every election.
Since he'd come of age, anyway.
Right here, in Washington County.
Always at the church on Maple Street.
He'd never missed… not one of 'em.
You can check the records on that.

He went for Franklin D. Roosevelt
for that unprecedented third term
just before World War II hit home.
He'd hated Nixon like everyone else,
tolerated Reagan, but figured Bush II
to be the beginning of America's end.

And now his kids want him to move
to the big city, three counties over,
in order to be closer to them. But…
where's he supposed to vote, he asks,
in the middle of that God-awful mess.
Lord, have mercy on his dying soul…

Of course, what choice does he have…
when it comes to his kids. They're good
kids… they're taking good care of him.
Besides, when it comes to this year's
front-runners… in either party…
what's left to vote for anyway?

"Why am I still here,"
she asks her daughters
when they visit the home?

"God must be busy," she says,
"what with the number of people
there are in the world these days."

"But Lord, surely he sees the mess
I am in, since the only thing I have
left to do is call his attention to it."

"No sir… he has forgotten me…
just like he forgot that other lady
in the south of France. She lived
to 127, have mercy on my soul."

"And hers."

"So… promise me, sweeties,
if this goes on much longer,
slip a little somethin'
into my tea."

99 – ONE MORE TIME

Secured, in his seat
in the bright little car
with wheels, he smiles,

faintly, and wonders why
the idea hadn't occurred
to him before now:

If life, after all,
is just one long
rollercoaster ride,

then why couldn't he,
when it comes to a stop,
simply unbuckle, get off…

go back…

and get in line again.

100 YEARS

Is she a culmination
   of all those days?
Over 36,000 of them?

Only the ones she recalls?
Or do the days she's forgotten
altogether, count for even more?

Do the days on which she was loved
add up to any less... or maybe more...
than the days on which she returned it?

How many of the wars she lived through
ended up never accomplishing anything?
And, how many sitting U.S. Presidents
did not make a difference, in the end?

Would a thousand extra summer days,
or winter nights by a warm fireplace,
ever hold a candle to that one, hot,
spring night she first made love?

Could the days she has left
be worth just as much
as all of the others
put together?

AUTHOR BIO

Nathan Brown is an author, songwriter, and award-winning poet currently living in Wimberley, Texas.

He holds a PhD in English and Journalism from the University of Oklahoma and has taught there for over twenty years. He also served as Poet Laureate for the State of Oklahoma in 2013 and 2014.

Nathan has published roughly nineteen books. Among them is *Don't Try*, a collection of poems co-written with songwriter and Austin Music Hall-of-Famer, Jon Dee Graham. His *Oklahoma Poems* anthology was a finalist for the Oklahoma Book Award. *Karma Crisis: New and Selected Poems* was a finalist for the Paterson Poetry Prize and the Oklahoma Book Award. His earlier book, *Two Tables Over*, won the 2009 Oklahoma Book Award. He has also released several CDs of original music.

For more, go to: **brownlines.com**

MEZCALITA
PRESS

An independent publishing company
dedicated to bringing the printed poetry,
fiction, and non-fiction of musicians who
want to add to the power and reach
of their important voices.